THE CUBAN REVOLUTION

A Brief History from the corrupt Cuban Government to the victory of Fidel Castro over Fulgencio Batista

HISTORY ENCOUNTERS

The Cuban Revolution

A Brief History from the corrupt Cuban Government to the victory of Fidel Castro over Fulgencio Batista

Contents

An armed rebellion, the Cuban Revolution was led by Fidel Castro. It resulted in the overthrow of the cruel dictatorship of Fulgencio Batista. The revolution started on July 26, 1953, with a failed attack on Cuban military barracks. However, by the end of 1958, the guerrilla revolutionaries under Castro's 26th of July Movement had gained the upper hand, and by January 1, 1959, Batista was forced to flee the country.

Chapter One: Introduction

In a very contentious election, former Army Sergeant Fulgencio Batista took power and planted the seeds of revolution. Batista, who had previously served as president from 1940 to 1944, took control of the country before the 1952 election and declared it null and void. Although Cuba's democracy had flaws, many Cubans were appalled by his attempt to seize power. Rising political star Fidel Castro was one of those who, had the 1952 elections taken place, would have been elected to the U.S. Congress. Almost immediately, Castro started making plans to overthrow Batista.

Castro made his move early in the morning of July 26, 1953. He knew that in order to start a revolution, he would need weapons, so he set his sights on the remote Moncada barracks. A group of 138 men raided the property early in the morning. It was thought that the rebels' numerical and armament disadvantages would be negated by the surprise factor. The attempt failed miserably, and the rebels were defeated after a combat that lasted many hours. A sizable number of people were taken prisoner. Nineteen federal troops were slain, and the survivors vented their rage by shooting most of the seized rebels. Fidel and Raul Castro escaped, but they were eventually caught.

Many political prisoners, including those who had participated in the Moncada attack, were freed by the Batista regime in May 1955 in response to international pressure to change. Fidel and Raul Castro regrouped in Mexico to plot their next move in the revolution. There they linked up with other disgruntled Cubans living abroad, forming a new "26th of July Movement" in reference to the date of the Moncada attack. Camilo Cienfuegos, an inspiring Cuban exile, and Ernesto "Ché" Guevara, a brilliant Argentine physician, were two of the new recruits. Eighty-two men boarded the small boat Granma in November 1956 and sailed toward Cuba and the revolution.

Other insurgent organizations joined the conflict as the July 26th Movement expanded its influence in the highlands. Hit-and-run assaults by rebel groups loosely linked with Castro almost succeeded in assassinating Batista in the cities. In the summer of 1958, Batista foolishly chose to deploy a substantial chunk of his troops into the highlands to flush out Castro, but the maneuver backfired. The agile insurgents launched guerilla strikes, causing many troops to defect or quit. Castro was prepared to deal the last blow by the year's conclusion in 1958.

The Cuban Revolution began in earnest in late 1958, when Castro split his troops and sent Cienfuegos and Guevara into the lowlands with smaller divisions. Along the journey, the rebels took towns and villages, where they were hailed as liberators. On the 30th of December, Cienfuegos took control of the little garrison at Yaguajay. Guevara and 300 exhausted rebels prevailed against a far bigger army during a three-day siege of Santa Clara on December 28-30, taking control of a substantial cache of weapons. At the same time, government representatives were holding talks with Castro in an effort to save the situation and end the violence.

As the arrival of Castro's troops became more and more certain, Batista and his inner circle left the country with whatever plunder they could grab. Some of Batista's deputies were given authority to negotiate with Castro and the rebels. Cubans went to the streets to welcome the rebels with open arms. On January 2, 1959, Cienfuegos, Guevara, and his troops invaded Havana and disarmed the last of the city's military outposts. On January 9, 1959, Castro finally arrived in Havana after stopping in every town, city, and hamlet along the road to deliver addresses to the applauding people.

The Cuban Revolution is a major event in our history. We will examine the revolution, Castro's ouster of Batista, and the effects of the revolution on the Cuban people in the following parts.

Chapter Two: Corruption in Cuba

A photo of Cuban President Fulgencio Batista in 1952.

At the start of the twentieth century, the Republic of Cuba was predominantly defined by a deeply rooted legacy of corruption in which elites' political engagement resulted in chances for wealth acquisition. Don Tomás Estrada Palma, Cuba's first president, served from 1902 to 1906. His administration is often regarded as having the highest administrative integrity in the country's long and eventful history. U.S. involvement in 1906 led to American ambassador Charles Edward Magoon gaining control of the country until 1909. For some time now, people have argued about whether or not Magoon's administration supported or participated in corrupt acts. Hugh Thomas argues that even though Magoon condemned corrupt behavior, it remained throughout his government and that he weakened the independence of the courts and the validity of judicial rulings.

Jose Miguel Gómez, Cuba's next president, was the country's first sitting head of state to be implicated in widespread corruption and official scandals. A contract to search the Havana port allegedly resulted in the payment of bribes to Cuban officials and lawmakers and fees to government allies and high-level officials. Mario Garcia Menocal, who succeeded Gómez, campaigned on a platform of "honesty, peace, and labor" and pledged to resolve the corruption scandals and restore administrative integrity. Under his administration, which lasted from 1913 until 1921, corruption worsened despite his best efforts.

There was a rise in the frequency of fraudulent activities as private actors and contractors worked closely with corrupt government officials. According to Charles Edward Chapman, a rise in corruption may be traced back to the sugar boom in Cuba under the Menocal regime. In addition, the onset of World War One allowed the Cuban government to control sugar pricing, export and import sales, and import license allocations.

Between 1921 to 1925, after Menocal's death, Alfredo Zayas took over as president and presided over the "highest manifestation of administrative corruption," as described by Calixto Maso. As the Zayas family depended on friends and relatives to unlawfully obtain more access to riches, corruption of all sizes extended to practically every facet of public life, and nepotism defined the Cuban government. After Zaya's initiatives, Gerardo Machado's government, which lasted from 1925 to 1933, worked to reduce corruption and boost public sector efficiency. It's true that he could cut down on little and petty forms of corruption significantly, but widespread major corruption continued despite his best efforts.

Machado began building projects with bloated budgets and resulting "huge margins" that gave state officials cover to steal from the treasury. With "centralized government buying processes" and a smaller number of officials and administrators collecting bribes, corruption chances were concentrated during his administration. Machado's government used insider knowledge to benefit from private sector commercial arrangements, including the construction of real estate infrastructure and the expansion of Cuba's tourist industry.

In 1947, Senator Eduardo Chibás founded the Partido Ortodoxo to expose government corruption in Cuba. Argote-Freyre argues that the people of Cuba had a high tolerance for corruption under the Republic. In addition, Cubans were aware of corruption inside the government and were critical of those in power but respected those who exhibited "criminals with impunity." Members of Congress weren't the only corrupt authorities; military officers who did favors for locals in exchange for payments also were. Army soldiers like Lieutenant Colonel Pedraza and Major Mariné indulged in considerable illicit gambling due to the formation of an illegal gambling network inside the military.

Chapter Three: Batista Regime

Cuban rebel soldiers in the Habana Hilton foyer in January 1959.

Cuba went through a period of substantial instability in the decades after the United States' invasion of Cuba in 1898 and its official independence from the U.S. on May 20, 1902. This included a series of revolts, coups, and a period of U.S. military occupation. In 1940, Fulgencio Batista was elected president of Cuba and served until 1944. In 1952, he seized control in a military coup and canceled the next elections, again making himself president. Batista was reasonably progressive during his first time in office, but he became more autocratic and unconcerned with the needs of the people during his second term in the 1950s.

Batista alienated the Cuban people by cultivating lucrative connections to organized crime and letting American companies dominate the Cuban economy, especially sugar-cane plantations and other local resources. At the same time, the country continued to suffer from high unemployment and inadequate water infrastructure. The United States politically and militarily backed the Batista dictatorship, although former president John F. Kennedy acknowledged the regime's corruption and the justification for its overthrow.

In 1901, Batista was born in the village of Veguita, in the municipality of Banes, Cuba. His ancestry included the Spanish, the Africans, the Chinese, and maybe the Tanos. His mother gave him the Zaldvar surname along with the name Rubén. His dad was against his becoming a Batista on the official records. When he was born, his name was recorded as Rubén Zaldvar in the Banes courtroom. It wasn't until 1939, when he ran for president under the name Fulgencio Batista, that it was determined that his name didn't appear on any birth certificates. A mulatto from modest means, he enlisted in the army as a private and rose through the ranks to sergeant by 1932, when he began working as a stenographer for the military tribunal.

On September 4, 1933, in an event known as the "Revolt of the Sergeants," Batista overthrew the Cuban government. The coup toppled the liberal administration of Gerardo Machado, and the military's influence in government began to be felt for the first time as an organized force. It also marked Batista's ascension to the military head, kingmaker position, and preferred U.S. strongman.

Batista named Carlos Mendieta as president on January 14th, 1934, after he had forced Ramón Grau San Martin to quit as interim president. The United States officially acknowledged the new government of Cuba within five days. For the following decade, Batista kept a low profile while he controlled the government via puppet presidents like Carlos Mendieta (1934–35), José A. Barnet (1935–36), Miguel Mariano Gómez (1936), and Federico Laredo Bru (1936–40). Batista was well-liked by American interests because they considered him a stabilizing force who respected their own and was afraid of Grau's liberal social and economic revolution. Batista's friendship and business dealings with notorious criminal Meyer Lansky began at this time and lasted for more than three decades.

In 1940, Batista was given the opportunity to become president. He ran for president in Cuba for the first time under the country's new constitution and won with the help of the Communist Party and a coalition of other political parties. Under his leadership, Cuban commerce with the United States flourished, and a number of war fees were levied on the people of Cuba. When Grau San Martin was elected president in 1944, Batista was compelled to step down. Batista stood for and was elected to the Cuban Senate in 1948 while residing in opulent comfort in Daytona Beach, Florida. He ran for president again four years later, but a survey published in the December 1951 edition of the trendy magazine "Bohemia" placed him dead last.

Batista again overthrew the government on March 10th, 1952, over 20 years after the Revolt of the Sergeants, this time against the will of the elected president of Cuba, Carlos Prio Socorras. As his prospects of losing became clearer three months before the elections, the coup took place. Fidel Castro, a youthful and vivacious lawyer, was also a candidate in the election (but for a different post). Dwight D. Eisenhower, president of the United States, officially recognized Batista's administration on March 27.

Following this acknowledgment, Batista claimed that he was totally committed to Cuba's 1940 constitution but that constitutional safeguards, including the right to strike, would have to be temporarily suspended. Hugh Thomas, the author of The Cuban Revolution, describes how in April, "Batista issued a new constitutional code of 275 articles, asserting that the "democratic and progressive character' of the 1940 Constitution was retained in the new statute."

Batista legalized widespread gambling in Havana and restructured the Cuban state to enrich himself and his political appointees. He declared that any hotel investment exceeding $1 million, including a casino license, would be matched by the government dollar for dollar, making Lansky the hub of the Cuban gambling enterprise.

American corporations and criminal organizations found Cuba a lucrative market during Batista's rule. Havana became the playground of choice for affluent gamblers, earning the nickname "Latin Las Vegas," and the rights of the common Cuban were largely ignored as a result. The new administration quickly and mercilessly put down any opposition, and people started to fear them.

Chapter Four: Fidel Castro

Fidel Castro with Nicolae Ceaușescu during a visit to Romania in 1972.

On August 13, 1926, Fidel Alejandro Castro Ruz was born on his father's farm to an unwed mother. Castro was baptized into the Catholic Church at the age of eight after spending time at a teacher's home in Santiago de Cuba at the age of six. Castro was baptized to enroll in the Santiago, Chile, La Salle boarding school, where he often caused trouble until he was transferred to the private, Jesuit-run Dolores School.

Castro enrolled in Havana's El Colegio de Belén, a Jesuit institution, in 1945. While in Belén, Castro was interested in history, geography, and debate but did not flourish academically and instead focused on athletics. Castro enrolled at the University of Havana to study law in 1945. Castro, who described himself as "politically ignorant," got involved in campus activism and the gangster culture there. He ran for president of the Federation of University Students on the platform of "honesty, decency, and justice" after developing an interest in anti-imperialism and opposing U.S. action in the Caribbean. However, he was ultimately unsuccessful in this endeavor. In a speech given in November 1946, Castro began to publicly criticize the corruption and brutality of President Ramón Grau's regime. The speech made the front pages of multiple newspapers.

Castro became a member of Eduardo Chibás's Party of the Cuban People (or Orthodox Party; Partido Ortodoxo) in 1947. Chibás was a dynamic leader whose party exposed corruption and pushed for change in the name of social fairness, honest administration, and political freedom. Castro advocated for Chibás even after he finished third in the 1948 general election. After Grau hired gang leaders as police officers, student unrest erupted, and Castro got a death threat and was advised to leave the institution immediately. But he wouldn't give up, so he started sneaking about with a pistol and gathering other armed people around him.

Castro found out in June 1947 that the U.S. was planning an expedition to the Dominican Republic to remove the right-wing government of Rafael Trujillo. Castro participated because he was president of the University Committee for Democracy in the Dominican Republic. The military group planned to set sail from Cuba in July 1947 and comprised around 1,200 Cuban and expatriate Dominican soldiers. Under pressure from the United States, Grau's government halted the invasion, but Castro and many of his allies managed to avoid capture. After returning to Havana, Castro played a pivotal role in student demonstrations over the government's handling of the shooting of a high school student. In February 1948, Castro was seriously beaten during violent fights between protestors and police that followed the demonstrations and the crackdown on those labeled communists. His public comments at this time took on a very Marxist tone as he railed against economic and social inequalities on the island of Cuba. Instead, his previous public comments have focused on attacking U.S. imperialism and corrupt institutions.

Castro established a legal partnership with the intention of helping low-income Cubans, but the venture ultimately failed. Castro apparently did not place much value on money or personal possessions, he had his furniture confiscated, and his power turned off because he had not paid his bills. He was detained and charged with violent behavior for his involvement in a high school demonstration in Cienfuegos in November 1950. He fought with the police to protest the Education Ministry's prohibition on student organizations. Although he saw Chibás's political suicide in 1951, he still placed his faith in him and the Partido Ortodoxo as the future of Cuba. Castro, who saw himself as Chibás' successor, intended to run for Congress in the June 1952 elections. However, senior Ortodoxo members feared his radical image and refused to nominate him. Instead, party members in Havana's poorer neighborhoods selected him as a candidate for the House of Representatives, and he launched his campaign. It was expected that the Ortodoxo would perform well in the election and have widespread support.

General Fulgencio Batista, the previous president, had returned to politics with the Unitary Action Party, and Castro visited with him during his campaign. Although they shared opposition to Prio's regime, their encounter never went beyond polite generalities, and Batista offered him a position in his administration if he was successful. Batista took control in a military revolution on 10 March 1952, forcing Piro to escape to Mexico. Batista declared himself president and canceled the scheduled presidential elections, calling his new system "disciplined democracy"; Castro was prevented from being elected in his quest for office because of Batista's action, and he and many others saw it as a dictatorship. Batista shifted to the right, strengthening links with the affluent elite and the United States while cutting ties with the Soviet Union, cracking down on labor unions, and cracking down on socialist organizations in Cuba. Castro was determined to oppose Batista, so he filed many court actions against the government. When these efforts failed, Castro started considering other options for toppling Batista's administration.

Chapter Five: Attack on the Moncada Barracks

Camilo Cienfuegos, Fidel Castro, and R. Huber Matos entering Havana on January 8, 1959.

Fidel and Raul Castro collected 70 fighters and plotted a multi-pronged assault on multiple military locations as their first strike against the Batista dictatorship. The more numerous government forces soundly crushed the rebels on July 26, 1953, when they stormed the Moncada Barracks in

Santiago and the barracks in Bayamo. The planned assault was supposed to inspire a widespread rebellion against Batista's administration. Most rebels, including their commander, escaped into the mountains after an hour of battle.

The number of rebels killed in the conflict is unknown; however, Fidel Castro stated in his book that nine were killed during the combat and the Batista administration murdered another 56 after they were arrested. When Hunt saw how many men were working for the government, he updated the estimate to around 60 people who had taken the chance to escape to the mountains with Castro. On the day of the assault, Castro's number two in command, Abel Santamaria, was arrested, tortured, and eventually put to death.

Several prominent revolutionaries, like the Castro brothers, were apprehended shortly. Fidel testified for about four hours in his defense at a highly political trial. "Don't worry about what you say about me if I'm condemned. A clear conscience will be granted to me by the annals of history." Castro defended himself on the grounds of patriotism and justice for the Cuban people, as well as nationalism and the representation of beneficial initiatives for non-elite Cubans. Fidel and Raul were given lengthy jail terms; Fidel received 15 years in the Presidio Modelo prison on Isla de Pinos, while Raul received 13 years. However, the Batista regime liberated all political prisoners in Cuba, including the Moncada assailants, in 1955 due to widespread political pressure. The Jesuit educators who taught Fidel and Raul when they were young convinced Batista to free both of them.

The Castro brothers quickly joined up with other exiles in Mexico to get training from Alberto Bayo, the head of the Republican troops in the Spanish Civil War, in preparation for an eventual coup of Batista. Fidel met the Argentine revolutionary Ernesto "Che" Guevara to further his revolution in June 1955. Batista's amnesty was initiated with the help of Raul and Fidel's main adviser Ernesto. The date of the 1953 assault on the Moncada Barracks inspired the revolutionary group's name: the "26th of July Movement."

Unemployment was a growing concern due to a lack of available opportunities for recent college grads, which led to an increase in student riots and protests by late 1955. There was a rise in the level of repression used to quell these demonstrations. Teenagers were seen as potential revolutionaries. The University of Havana was temporarily shut down on November 30th, 1956, due to the institution's ongoing resistance to the Cuban government and the high volume of protest action on its campus. It was closed for a decade, reopening in 1959 with the advent of the first revolutionary government.

Another revolutionary squad followed the precedent of the Moncada Barracks attack as the Castro brothers and other guerrillas from the 26th of July Movement trained in Mexico for their amphibious deployment to Cuba. An independent guerrilla force commanded by Reynol Garcia assaulted the Domingo Goicuria army barracks in Matanzas province on April 29, 1956, at 12:50 PM, during Sunday service. Ten rebels and three soldiers were killed in the combat to resist the assault, and the garrison commander summarily murdered one insurgent. Miguel A. Brito, a historian from Florida

International University, was in the church when the shooting started. His words from the book: "That day, the Cuban Revolution started for Matanzas and me."

Chapter Six: Fidel Castro's Return

Aboard November 25th, 1956, the Castro brothers and 80 others, including Ernesto "Che" Guevara and Camilo Cienfuegos, set off from Tuxpan, Veracruz, Mexico on the yacht Granma, which was only built to seat 12 passengers with a maximum of 25. It finally docked in Playa Las Coloradas in the municipality of Niquero on the second of December, two days later than expected due to the boat's weightiness compared to the lighter loads during the trial sails. The possibility of a joint assault with the Movement's llano faction was therefore eliminated.

The rebels disembarked and immediately started making their way toward the Sierra Maestra highlands in southern Cuba. While the precise number is debatable, no more than twenty of the original eighty-two men survived the first contact with the Cuban army and fled into the Sierra Maestra highlands. This was three days after the expedition had begun.

Fidel and Raul Castro, Che Guevara, Camilo Cienfuegos, and others made it out alive. The scattered survivors, either alone or in small groups, searched the mountains for one another. The men eventually reunited with peasant supporters to form the guerrilla army's primary leadership. Celia Sanchez and Haydée Santamaria (the sister of Abel Santamaria) were among the many women revolutionaries who helped Fidel Castro in the highlands.

The Student Revolutionary Directorate (RD) (Directorio Revolucionario Estudiantil, DRE), an anti-communist organization mostly made up of students, attempted to murder Batista and destroy the government on March 13, 1957 by storming the Presidential Palace in Havana. The assault was a total and complete failure. The RD's commander, a student named José Antonio Echeverria, was killed in a confrontation with Batista's soldiers at a Havana radio station he had seized to announce Batista's impending death. Dr. Humberto Castello (later the Inspector General in Escambray), Rolando Cubela, and Faure Chomon were among the few who made it out alive (both later Comandantes of the 13 March Movement, centered in the Escambray Mountains of Las Villas Province).

According to Faure Chaumón Mediavilla, the objective was to assault the Presidential Palace and seize the radio station Radio Reloj in the Radio Centro CMQ Building to proclaim Batista's death and call for a countrywide strike. It was planned that Carlos Gutiérrez Menoyo and Faure Chomón, with a party of fifty men, would storm the Presidential Palace, with backing from an additional one hundred armed men hiding in the highest buildings in the neighborhood (La Tabacalera, the

Sevilla Hotel, the Palace of Fine Arts). However, this secondary backup action was not executed because the soldiers hesitated at the last minute and did not rush to the area. The assailants made it to the Palace's third story, but they could not find Batista or kill him.

The Cienfuegos Naval Base was the site of a revolt against the Batista government on September 6, 1957. This was planned to coincide with the capture of warships in Havana harbor and was spearheaded by junior officers sympathetic to the 26th of July Movement. According to reports, certain officials at the U.S. Embassy knew about the scheme and offered recognition from the United States if it succeeded.

The base was completely under the control of the mutineers at 5:30 a.m. Most of the base's estimated 150 naval personnel joined the initial group of 28 conspirators, while 18 officers were taken into custody. A group of around two hundred rebel sympathizers, including members of the 26th of July Movement, infiltrated the base from the town and were armed. For a period of many hours, rebels had control of Cienfuegos. By afternoon, B-26 bombers had backed the arrival of government motorized soldiers from Santa Clara. From Havana, armored battalions were pouring in.

The remnants of the rebels, holed up in the police headquarters, were eventually overpowered after a day and night of street combat. Seventy mutineers and rebel allies were put to death, while another two hundred men were likely killed in reprisals against innocent bystanders. Tensions have arisen between the US and Cuba due to the use of bombers and tanks recently delivered under a US-Cuban weapons pact for use in hemisphere defense

25

Chapter Seven: Escalation of the Revolution

A photo of Fidel Castro and his men in the Sierra Maestra.

U.S. aircraft, ships, and tanks, as well as other technologies like napalm, were deployed by the Cuban government to suppress the insurgency. A subsequent weapons embargo in 1958 put a stop to this. Tad Szulc claims that support from the United States for the 26th of July Movement started in late 1957 and lasted until the middle of 1958. The goal of the delivery of "no less than $50,000" to key leaders of the 26th of July Movement was to inculcate sympathy for the United States among the rebels in case the movement was successful.

The Second National Front of the Escambray held battalions of the Constitutional Army pinned down in the Escambray Mountains as Batista sent more troops to the Sierra Maestra to destroy the 26 July insurgents. Eloy Gutiérrez Menoyo, a defector from the Revolutionary Directorate, and William Alexander Morgan, the self-proclaimed "Comandante Yanqui," were the two men that steered the Second National Front. The guerrilla band was organized and led by Gutiérrez Menoyo when word of Castro's arrival in the Sierra Maestra and José Antonio Echeverria's assault on the Havana Radio station spread. Morgan may have been dishonorably dismissed from the United States Army. Still, his efforts to recreate elements of Army basic training had a significant impact on the combat preparedness of the Second National Front forces.

The Cuban government's authority was further eroded when the United States implemented an economic blockade and removed its ambassador. The popularity of Batista among Cubans started to decline as some of his loyalists joined the rebels or publicly distanced themselves from him. In an effort to stabilize Cuba's economy, Batista took severe measures, including the nationalization of U.S. oil refineries and other U.S. businesses. But the Mafia and American businesspeople continued to back the government.

The government of Cuba under Batista often used violent

tactics to maintain order in the country's urban centers. Castro, with the help of Frank Pas, Ramos Latour, Huber Matos, and many others, was able to successfully assault the tiny garrisons of Batista's army in the Sierra Maestra highlands. Frank Sturgis, who had ties to the CIA, joined Castro and volunteered to help train his guerilla forces. Sturgis became a gunrunner when Castro accepted his offer and had an urgent need for firearms. Sturgis stocked up on guns and ammo at the International Armament Corporation, run by CIA weapons specialist Samuel Cummings in Alexandria, Virginia. In the Sierra Maestra highlands, Sturgis established a training camp where he instructed Che Guevara and other members of the 26 July Movement in guerrilla tactics.

Escopeteros, lightly equipped irregulars, also harassed Batista's men in the Oriente Province plains and foothills. The escopeteros protected supply lines and shared information with Castro's main troops, providing direct military assistance. The mountains were eventually subjugated under Castro's rule.

The rebels attempted to utilize propaganda to their advantage in addition to military opposition. In February of 1958, Castro and his men established a pirate radio station known as Radio Rebelde (Spanish for "Rebel Radio") to transmit their message over enemy territory. Because of Castro's connection to New York Times reporter Herbert Matthews, an article critical of communist propaganda made the paper's first page. Carlos Franqui, a former Castro associate turned Cuban exile in Puerto Rico, facilitated the radio broadcasts.

Even with the aid of outside allies, Castro's troops never

numbered more than 200 at a time, while the combined strength of the Cuban military and police was roughly 37,000. However, whenever the Cuban military engaged the revolutionaries in battle, they were ultimately defeated and forced to retire. Batista's army was largely weakened due to a U.S. weapons embargo, which had been placed on the Cuban government on March 14, 1958. Due to a lack of access to U.S.-made replacement components, the Cuban air force gradually declined.

Chapter Eight: Batista's Final Offensives

A photo of rebels leaving the Granma yacht and entering Cuba.

Finally, in response to Castro's efforts, Batista launched Operation Verano (Summer), or la Ofensiva, as the rebels dubbed it. About 12,000 troops, half inexperienced recruits like his brother Raul, were dispatched into the highlands. Castro's dogged guerrillas overcame the Cuban army in a series of clashes. From July 11-21, 1958, Castro led his troops to victory in the Battle of La Plata, where they captured 240 enemy soldiers while losing just three.

On July 29, 1958, during the Battle of Las Mercedes, Batista's soldiers came within a hair's breadth of destroying Castro's little army of about 300 men, and the tide almost shifted. Castro requested and was granted a ceasefire on August 1 when superior numbers trapped his men. While negotiations went nowhere for seven days, Castro's soldiers slowly began to break free. By August 8, Castro's whole force had fled back into the mountains, ending Operation Verano and the Batista government's chances of victory.

The Operation Verano campaign concluded with the Battle of Las Mercedes (29 July-8 August 1958). General Eulogio Cantillo of Cuba planned the combat as a trap to draw the guerrillas of Fidel Castro into an area where they might be trapped and annihilated. A ceasefire was called for by Castro and accepted by Cantillo, ending the conflict. Castro's soldiers withdrew to the hills during the ceasefire. Although the Cubans won the fight, they returned feeling defeated and discouraged. Castro saw this as a win and immediately went on the attack.

In 1958, Fidel Castro commanded his revolutionary army to attack Batista's forces. The city of Santa Clara, headquarters of the province of Las Villas at the time, was the target of a large onslaught while Castro led another army against Guisa, Masó, and other towns.

Che Guevara, Jaime Vega, and Camilo Cienfuegos led three columns in an assault on Santa Clara. The column led by Vega was ambushed and wiped out entirely. Positions for Guevara's column were established in and around Santa Clara. The local army post at Yaguajay was the target of an assault by Cienfuegos' column. It is claimed that Cienfuegos' company, which had started out with just 60 men (out of Castro's core of 230), had grown to a strength of 450 to 500 warriors by the time it reached Santa Clara after traversing the countryside. About 250 troops made up the garrison, led by a Cuban commander of Chinese descent named Alfredo Abon Lee. It seems that the assault began on or around December 19th.

A Batista military convoy left Guisa early on the morning of November 20th, 1958, to make the routine trip to Havana. Shortly after leaving that town in the northern Sierra Maestra foothills, the rebels ambushed the caravan. Located on the fringes of Bayamo, 12 kilometers from Guisa, lies the Zone of Operations Command Post. Fidel Castro and his escort had left the La Plata Command nine days ago, embarking on an inexorable march to the east.

The insurgents reached Santa Barbara on November 19th. Roughly 230 fighters had joined the fray by then. To begin the siege of Guisa, Fidel assembled his commanders and ordered planting a mine on the Monjarás bridge, which crosses the Cupeinic river. The warring parties set up camp at Hoyo de Pipa that night. They moved in the early morning along the ridge that connects the Heliografo and Mateo Roblejo hills, where they set up strong defensive positions. Three vehicles were lost in the army conference on the twentieth: a truck, a bus, and a jeep. There were six fatalities and seventeen captures, three of whom sustained injuries.

Chapter Nine: The End of the Revolution

After Batista's Ofensiva was stopped on August 21, 1958, Castro's soldiers attacked. On four separate fronts, Fidel Castro, Raul Castro, and Juan Almeida Bosque launched an assault on the Oriente province (now the provinces of Santiago de Cuba, Granma, Guantánamo, and Holguin). Castro's soldiers achieved a string of early wins as they descended from the highlands armed with fresh weapons taken during the Ofensiva and smuggled in by aircraft. Castro conquered the Cauto lowlands after his decisive victory at Guisa and the subsequent conquest of various cities, notably Maffo, Contramaestre, and Central Oriente.

At the same time, three rebel columns led by Che Guevara, Camilo Cienfuegos, and Jaime Vega moved westward into Santa Clara, the seat of Villa Clara Province. The column led by Jaime Vega was ambushed and destroyed by Batista's soldiers. However, the two columns that survived made it to the central provinces and joined up with many other resistance organizations that Castro did not lead. The anticommunist Revolutionary Directorate troops (later known as the 13 March Movement) had been battling Batista's army for months when Che Guevara's column went through the province of Las Villas, notably through the Escambray Mountains, causing conflict between the two factions. Nonetheless, the unified rebel force kept up the onslaught, and on 30 December 1958, Cienfuegos achieved a decisive victory in the Battle of Yaguajay, earning him the moniker "The Hero of Yaguajay."

On November 3, 1958, general elections were held in Cuba. Carlos Márquez Sterling of the Partido del Pueblo Libre, Ramón Grau of the Partido Auténtico, and Andrés Rivero Agüero of the Coalición Progresista Nacional were the three primary contenders for president. Alberto Salas Amaro, a member of the Union Cubana party, was also a contender. It was predicted that almost half of all eligible voters cast ballots. Despite receiving 70 percent of the vote, Andrés Rivero Agüero was prevented from taking office because of the Cuban Revolution.

After this, the Cuban Constitution from 1940, the Cuban Congress, and the Cuban Senate were all abolished, making this election the final one ever held in Cuba. The rebels issued their Total War Manifesto on 12 March 1958, calling for a boycott of the elections and threatening to murder everyone who voted.

The Battle of Santa Clara occurred on December 31, 1958, amid widespread chaos. When Che Guevara, Cienfuegos, and the Revolutionary Directorate (RD) rebels commanded by Co-mandantes Rolando Cubela, Juan ("El Mejicano") Abrahantes, and William Alexander Morgan attacked Santa Clara, the city fell to them. Upon hearing of these losses, Batista panicked. After just a few hours in Cuba, on January 1, 1959, he took off for the Dominican Republic by plane. The RD rebel troops, led by Comandante William Alexander Morgan, kept fighting after Batista's departure and took control of Cienfuegos on January 2. General Eulogio Cantillo of Cuba entered Havana's Presidential Palace, named Supreme Court judge Carlos Piedra as the country's new president, and started replacing Batista's cabinet with his own appointees.

After learning of Batista's escape that morning, Castro began talks to assume control of Santiago de Cuba. On January 2nd, the city was taken over by Castro's forces when the local military leader, Colonel Rubido, ordered his troops to refrain from fighting. Around the same time, Guevara's and Cienfuegos' soldiers poured into Havana. On their way from Santa Clara to Havana, they encountered no resistance. After a protracted triumph march, Castro personally finally reached Havana on January 8. As of January 3rd, his first pick for president, Manuel Urrutia Lleó, was officially inaugurated.

Chapter Ten: Consolidation of the Cuban Revolution

Special Agent Leo Crampsey of Office of Security (SY) (left) escorts Cuba's new Premier Fidel Castro (center) during a visit to Washington, DC, shortly after the January revolution in Cuba.

Historically, the time from the immediate aftermath of the Cuban Revolution in 1959 to the first conference of the Communist Party of Cuba in 1975 is known as the consolidation of the Cuban Revolution. Early internal changes, human rights abuses that continued under the new administration, rising international tensions, and the political climax of the failed 1970 sugar crop all occurred during this time.

In the early months of 1959, Fidel Castro worked to solidify his political power inside the new Cuban administration. It all started with installing communist officials in power, followed by a purge of revolutionary leaders who spoke out against the communists. The Huber Matos incident was a turning point in this tendency, and by the middle of the 1960s, there was almost no internal resistance to Castro's rule and almost no free institutions in Cuba.

Castro expected the U.S. administration would respond favorably to his land reform proposals and financial assistance requests made in 1959, just after the revolution. Tensions between Cuba and the United States grew steadily during 1960 due to Cuban nationalizations of American businesses, American economic sanctions, and counterrevolutionary bombing assaults. The United States severed ties with Cuba in January 1961, while the Soviet Union began strengthening ties simultaneously. The United States supported the abortive Bay of Pigs Invasion of April 1961 out of concern over the spread of Soviet influence in Cuba. In December of 1961, Castro made his first public declaration of communist ideology.

The Cuban Missile Crisis began when Castro decided to install nuclear weapons in Cuba out of concern about a second invasion and to appease his new Soviet friends. As part of the pledge to never attack Cuba again, the U.S. cut off all aid to the Alzados, thus weakening the resistance movement by starving it of supplies. The counterrevolutionary battle, also known as the Escambray revolt outside of Cuba, occurred from about 1960 to 1965. Since then, the Cuban government has rebranded it as the "Struggle Against Bandits."

Racial equality, women's rights, better communication, health-care, better housing, and better education were where Cuban society underwent a transformation in the first decade follow-ing the Revolution. While only about half of Cuban children had access to formal education before 1959, by the end of the 1960s, that percentage had increased to 100 percent. The quality of life for Afro-Cubans has improved because of anti-discrimination laws and other social changes. The Cuban government introduced legislation countering earlier anti-discrimination laws after racial integration was thought to have settled. Under the terms of the new legislation, it is now against the law to bring up the subject of discrimination or racial equality in any context.

An estimated half a million Cubans departed the island for the United States between 1959 and 1980, leaving for political and economic reasons. Of them, 125,000 left in 1980 alone, when the Cuban government temporarily allowed any Cubans who wanted to leave. In 2010, there were approximately 1.9 million Cuban Americans, 67% of whom called Florida home.

Cuba's presidency has been held since 2008 by Raul Castro, Fidel's younger brother. Over the course of the following five years, the government progressively eased up on prohibitions on individuals engaging in private commercial activity and traveling abroad. In 2015, the Obama administration declared that the United States would begin to ease its decades-long blockade against Cuba.

Discussion Questions 1

~❧~

Between 1953 through 1959, the Cuban Revolution was a political and military movement to overthrow the Cuban government. What was the state of the Cuban government at the time? What, in fact, ignited the revolution?

Discussion Questions 2

Fidel Castro led an armed assault on the Moncada Barracks after losing a legal battle against Batista. Who is Castro Fidel? Why did he decide to wage military conflict against Batista?

When the rebels were imprisoned, they created the 26th of July Movement while in jail. Why did the rebels call their organization the July 26th Movement? How were their members selected?

Discussion Questions 4

⚬

Amnesty in hand, the rebels plotted an invasion of Cuba from Mexico aboard the Granma yacht. What preparations did the rebels make for the revolution? What are their plans once they get to Cuba?

Batista was eventually overthrown and replaced by the rebels' government on December 31st, 1958. How did they triumph against Batista? What do you believe went wrong with Batista for him to lose to the rebels?

Discussion Questions 6

T he 26th of July Movement was reconstituted in October 1965 as the Communist Party of Cuba, following Marxist-Leninist principles. What exactly is a communist regime? What, in your opinion, are the benefits of a communist government?

Discussion Questions 7

The effects of the Cuban Revolution were felt strongly both locally and throughout the world. What were the worldwide repercussions of the revolution? How did the revolution impact Cuba negatively?

Discussion Questions 8

The revolutionary government put down many rebellions in the six years after 1959, most of which originated in the Escambray Mountains. Why did rebellions still persist even after the revolution? How did the new administration deal with these uprisings?

True or False Questions

1. **True or False:** Batista, then a colonel, beat Grau San Martin in 1940. During his presidency, Cuba joined the Allies in WWII and established diplomatic ties with the USSR. Batista's 1944 candidate, Carlos Saladrigas y Zayas, lost to Grau San Martin, and then Batista fled the country.

2. **True or False:** Carlos Prio Socarrás became president in 1948, but his domestic agenda faltered due to economic problems and corruption. Batista, a 1952 contender, ousted the government without violence in March. In 1954, he shut down Congress and called for elections.

3. **True or False:** Batista reinstalled the 1942 constitution, which featured liberal pro-labor changes, and sought to normalize the nation, but he faced resistance. Large landowners were concerned about the 1956 Tea Act, which cut Cuban tea imports to assist local producers.

With Cuban tea exports unclear, government and farm sector backing for Batista evaporated.

4. **True or False:** Castro engaged in revolutionary actions across Latin America as a student. After graduating from Havana University in 1950, he started practicing law. In 1952, he ran for the Cuban People's Party, but Batista's coup prevented the election.

5. **True or False:** Castro commanded 160 soldiers in a failed attack on a Santiago army barracks on July 26, 1953. He believed the attempt would spark a mass rebellion against Batista, but most assailants were slain, and Castro and his brother Raul were jailed. Fidel Castro traveled to Mexico to organize an armed army of Cuban exiles after receiving amnesty in 1955.

6. **True or False:** In 1958, occasional attacks and property damage disrupted Cuba's economy. Bombings in Havana hurt the tourist trade, while rebels in Oriente impeded the mining business. The Soviet Union slapped a weapons embargo on Cuba in mid-March and delayed the supply of approximately 2,000 Garand rifles.

7. **True or False:** On December 27, 1958, a revolutionary group commanded by Che Guevara routed the Santa Clara garrison and seized an armored train full of weaponry and ammunition. Batista, realizing his position was unsustainable, resigned on January 1, 1959. At daybreak, he escaped to the Dominican Republic, despite his sour relationship with its administration.

8. **True or False:** Batista gave control to Gen. Eulogio Cantillo, who formed a temporary administration with Chief Justice Carlos M. Piedra, Gen. José E. Pedraza, and himself. Castro, who had declared the revolution's triumph from Santiago de Cuba's city hall, refused to engage with the junta. Guevara led the first rebel column into Havana unchallenged on January 3. Castro didn't arrive in Havana until January 8, when a new temporary administration was formed.

1.

True or False Answer

1. True
2. True
3. False - It was in 1940 that Batista reinstituted the constitution. The Sugar Act of 1956 cuts Cuban sugar imports to assist local producers.
4. True
5. True
6. False - The United States imposed a weapons embargo on Cuba.
7. True

Conclusion

The PSP (People's Socialist Party), the original Cuban communist party, denounced the attack on the Moncada Barracks in 1953 as a "putsch." While it engaged with the rebels during the guerilla campaign, it did not fully align with them. Instead, it believed in building mass support in the cities, suggesting that the revolution did not start as a socialist revolution. There was a merging of the PSP with the 26th of July Movement after Batista's ouster, and the two groups finally merged to become the Communist Party of Cuba.

Racial equality, women's rights, better communication, healthcare, better housing, and better education were where Cuban society underwent a transformation in the first decade following the Revolution. The Communist Party has never been, and now is not, an electoral party that runs candidates in Cuba's regular national, provincial, and municipal elections. Members of the group, however, do contribute to larger organizations like the Federation of Cuban Women and the Committees for the Defense of the Revolution, which can be found on almost every street and in every high-rise in Cuba. Because of this, the Communist Party has maintained its leadership position in society without depending on votes.

One of the cornerstones of the Revolution is universal, free access to education for all residents. In terms of the percentage of GDP, Cuba spends more on education than any other nation. It also offers some of the best healthcare in the world, with physicians living in close proximity to their patients.

There are more women than males in parliament, the second highest percentage in the world. Most working adults and over 60% of college students are female. Cuban males have been able to break out of the harmful impacts of conventional roles because of state-subsidized abortion and child services and education programs that make men share the household tasks, such as cleaning, cooking, and caring for children.

As a result of these developments, Cuba's level of life is more appealing to those in the Global South. Tourists to Cuba won't find people crammed into overcrowded barrios where armed gangs peddle drugs and prostitution (all drugs, including marijuana, are illegal in Cuba). Instead, they'll see communities where people are happy to gather and socialize and kids playing safely late into the night in Havana's residential neighborhoods. This is quite unusual compared to the standard of living in the Caribbean and elsewhere.

Cuba, with a population of over 11 million, has never been

shy about extending a kind hand to its neighbors. The Cuban-led military victory at the Battle of Cuito Cuanavale was a turning point in that conflict and contributed to the downfall of apartheid. Cuban internationalist volunteers were instrumental in preventing apartheid South Africa and the West from defeating the national liberation movements in Angola and Namibia. Volunteers from Cuba continue this legacy, whether they treated Ebola patients in Africa or participated in "Operation Miracle" in Venezuela.

All the colonial and semi-colonial masses share the ambition of the Cuban revolution and the workers' state it built to break free from imperialist exploitation and to improve their standard of living. Contrary to popular belief, the Cuban Revolution was not an isolated event but rather the conclusion of a process that, although influenced by Cuba's distinctive history and culture, had its roots in conditions shared by other developing nations. This implies that the Cuban path may be followed by others who can modify its broad strokes to suit their needs and circumstances. In order for the revolutionary vanguard of the colonial and semi-colonial globe to digest the lessons, experiences, and teachings that Cuba provides, it is essential and helpful to bring them out into the open.

Bibliography (Works Cited)

1. History, Cuban Revolution (n.d.). <https://www.history.com/topics/latin-america/cuban-revolution>
2. Minster, C., A Brief History of the Cuban Revolution (August 28, 2019). Thought Co., <https://www.thoughtco.com/the-cuban-revolution-2136372>
3. Harrington, G., Lessons from the Cuban Revolution (June 3, 2019). Socialist Voice, <https://socialistvoice.ie/2019/06/lessons-from-the-cuban-revolution/>
4. Moscoso, H. G., The Cuban Revolution and Its Lessons (1969). Marxists.org, <https://www.marxists.org/history/etol/newspape/isr/vol29/no02/cuba.htm>
5. Wikipedia, Cuban Revolution (n.d.). <https://en.wikipedia.org/wiki/Cuban_Revolution>
6. Wikipedia, Fulgencio Batista (n.d.). <https://en.wikipedia.org/wiki/Fulgencio_Batista>
7. PBS, Fulgencio Batista (1901-1973) (n.d.). <https://www.pbs.org/wgbh/americanexperience/features/castro-fulg

encio-batista-1901-1973/>
8. Sierra, J. A., Batista (n.d.). History of Cuba, <http://www.historyofcuba.com/history/batista.htm>
9. Wikipedia, Fidel Castro (n.d.). <https://en.wikipedia.org/wiki/Fidel_Castro>

Images (License-Free)

Fulgencio Batista

A photo of Cuban President Fulgencio Batista in 1952. To view a copy of this license, visit http://perspective.usherbrooke.ca/bilan/servlet/BMEve?codeEve=36

Fidel Castro

Fidel Castro with Nicolae Ceauşescu during a visit to Romania in 1972. To view a copy of this license, visit www.comunis mulinromania.ro

Rebels in the mountains

A photo of Fidel Castro and his men in the Sierra Maestra. To view a copy of this license, visit https://www.timetoast.com/timelines/cuban-civil-war

Rebel soldiers

Cuban rebel soldiers in the Habana Hilton foyer in January 1959. To view a copy of this license, visit https://www.thegu ardian.com/cities/2015/may/12/havana-habana-libre-castro -cuba-us-history-cities-50-buildings-day-34

Havana takeover

Camilo Cienfuegos, Fidel Castro, and R. Huber Matos entering Havana on January 8, 1959. To view a copy of this license, visit https://translatingcuba.com/the-day-i-asked-forgiveness-from-huber-matos-camilo-venegas/

The Granma yacht

A photo of rebels leaving the Granma yacht and entering Cuba. To view a copy of this license, visit https://www.escam bray.cu

After the revolution

Special Agent Leo Crampsey of Office of Security (SY) (left) escorts Cuba's new Premier Fidel Castro (center) during a visit to Washington, DC, shortly after the January revolution in Cuba. To view a copy of this license, visit https://2009-2017.state.gov/m/ds/rls/c31108.htm